SALAMANDERS

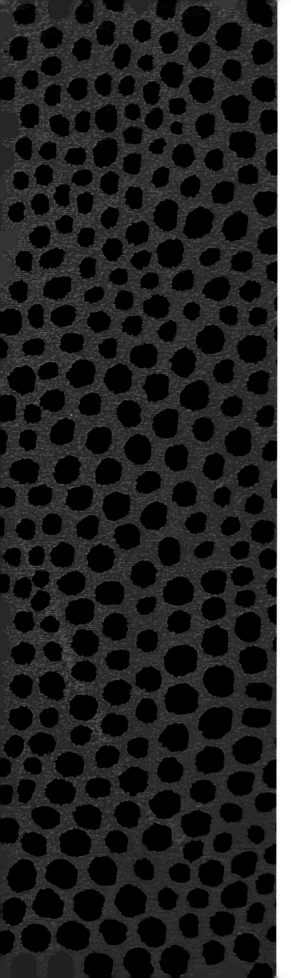

LIVING WILD

Published by Creative Education and Creative Paperbacks
P.O. Box 227, Mankato, Minnesota 56002
Creative Education and Creative Paperbacks are imprints of The Creative Company
www.thecreativecompany.us

Design and production by Mary Herrmann
Art direction by Rita Marshall
Printed in China

Photographs by Alamy (blickwinkel, Nature Picture Library), Creative Commons Wikimedia (Daiju Azuma, Babsy, Dr. Günter Bechly, Digitised Manuscripts/British Library, Ecelan, Giogo, Google Arts & Culture/The J. Paul Getty Museum, Brian Gratwicke/Flickr, harem.koh/Flickr, The High Fin Sperm Whale, Jim.henderson, KENPEI, Utagawa Kuniyoshi, Oregon Caves/Flickr, Oregon Department of Fish & Wildlife/Flickr, th1098, Thomon, Josiah H. Townsend/CalPhotos, United States Geological Survey, V31S70/Flickr), Dreamstime (Designpicssub, Jason P Ross), Getty Images (Suzanne L. & Joseph T. Collins), iStockphoto (Artistan, Derek_Neumann, JasonOndreicka, lisad1724, Snowleopard1, WitR), Shutterstock (avtor painter, Bildagentur Zoonar GmbH, Choke29, FABRIZIO CONTTE, domnitsky, Dirk Ercken, Jeff Holcombe, Vitalii Hulai, Rosa Jay, Matt Jeppson, Branko Jovanovic, Lapis2380, Marco Maggesi, Martha Marks, Marques, Jay Ondreicka, reptiles4all, trek6500, Louis W, Tim Zurowski)

Library of Congress Cataloging-in-Publication Data
Names: Gish, Melissa, author.
Title: Salamanders / Melissa Gish.
Series: Living wild.
Includes index.
Summary: A look at salamanders, including their habitats, physical characteristics such as their smooth, permeable skin, behaviors, relationships with humans, and the remarkable adaptability of these widespread amphibians today.
Identifiers: LCCN 2017038415 / ISBN 978-1-60818-961-8 (hardcover) / ISBN 978-1-62832-566-9 (pbk) / ISBN 978-1-64000-040-7 (eBook)

Subjects: LCSH: Salamanders—Juvenile literature.
Classification: LCC QL668.C2 G55 2018 / DDC 597.8/5—dc23

CCSS: RI.5.1, 2, 3, 8; RST.6-8.1, 2, 5, 6, 8; RH.6-8.3, 4, 5, 6, 7, 8

First Edition HC 9 8 7 6 5 4 3 2 1
First Edition PBK 9 8 7 6 5 4 3 2 1

CREATIVE EDUCATION • CREATIVE PAPERBACKS

SALAMANDERS

Melissa Gish

Amid a tangle of plants and algae-covered stones in
a Kansas wetland, a barred tiger salamander

is hunting by the light of a crescent moon. It spots a western chorus frog at the water's edge.

A mid a tangle of plants and algae-covered stones in a Kansas wetland, a barred tiger salamander is hunting by the light of a crescent moon. It spots a western chorus frog at the water's edge. The frog is also a nighttime predator, but now *it* is the one being stalked. The salamander creeps silently toward its prey. The young frog is just over an inch (2.5 cm) long—10 times smaller than the salamander—but it has the advantage of speed. If it detects the salamander, it will disappear in a flash. The salamander takes one slow step after another. Then it freezes. A small spider passes near the frog, and in an instant, the frog's tongue shoots forward to nab the unwary arachnid. The salamander takes advantage of the frog's distraction. In three quick strides, it grabs the frog in its powerful jaws. The salamander swallows its prey with a single gulp.

WHERE IN THE WORLD THEY LIVE

■ **Japanese Giant Salamander**
Japanese rivers

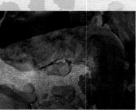

Chinese Giant Salamander
Chinese rivers

■ **Northern Spectacled Salamander**
Italian forests

Greater Siren
coastal plains from Maryland to Alabama

■ **Barred Tiger Salamander**
grasslands and forests from south-central Canada to northern Mexico

■ **Axolotl**
Mexico's Lake Xochimilco

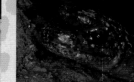

■ **Coastal Giant Salamander**
streams and forests from southern British Columbia to northern California

Varying from less than half an inch (1.3 cm) to six feet (1.8 m) in length, the more than 650 salamander species are primarily found in temperate climates throughout the Northern Hemisphere. While several species continue to flourish in their native habitats today, many others are critically endangered. The colored squares represent the locations of selected species in the wild today.

S alamanders are members of the Amphibia class of animals, which are characterized by living part of their lives in water and part on land. Salamanders can be found on every continent except Antarctica. They are related to toads, frogs, and limbless caecilians (*seh-SILL-yens*). Salamanders have **adapted** a variety of life-history patterns that allow them to survive in a wide range of habitats. Some are **aquatic**, breathing through **gills** lined with frilly filaments that take in oxygen from the water. Others are terrestrial, living on land. More than 650 salamander species comprise the order Caudata, from the Latin word for "tail," *cauda*. They are further divided into 10 families with incredibly diverse characteristics.

Some salamander families are fully aquatic, including the giant salamanders of Asia, which are the world's largest. The Chinese giant salamander can grow up to six feet (1.8 m) long, and the Japanese giant salamander can be five feet (1.5 m) long. The siren family, named for the **mythical** Greek creatures, is found only in the southeastern United States and Mexico. More than 50 members of the Asiatic salamander family inhabit much of Asia and parts of

Salamanders may seek out sunshine to warm up, but their bodies must remain moist at all times.

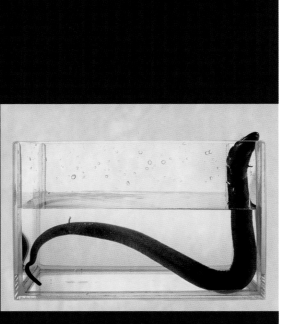

Despite their body length, Amphiumidae salamanders' legs are less than one inch (2.5 cm) long.

Special cells called macrophages help most salamanders regrow damaged limbs, tails, eye lenses, spinal cords, and even organ parts.

Russia, with about half found only in Japan. Members of the family Amphiumidae are sometimes mistakenly called "conger eels" because these salamanders burrow in mud and can move across wet ground to get from one water source to another—just like the eels. They range from 12 to 42 inches (30.5–107 cm) in length and are found only in the southeastern U.S.

In 1689, while exploring a cave in what is now Slovenia, naturalist Johann Weikhard von Valvasor discovered what he presented to the world as a baby dragon. Two decades later, Austrian naturalist Josephus Nicolaus Laurenti named the discovery *Proteus anguinus*, after the shapeshifting sea god Proteus. Today, this creature, called the olm, is found only in the underground waters of the Dinaric Alps in southeastern Europe. Other members of the fully aquatic Proteidae family are four waterdogs, found from Texas to North Carolina, and the mudpuppy, found throughout the eastern and midwestern U.S. and south-central Canada.

Other salamander families are terrestrial. The torrent salamanders are named for the fast-moving brooks and streams called torrents in the forests of California, Oregon, and Washington. The Pacific

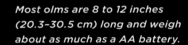

Most olms are 8 to 12 inches (20.3–30.5 cm) long and weigh about as much as a AA battery.

Female Pacific giant salamanders are known to fiercely defend their eggs from predators—including other salamanders.

giant salamanders are also named for their location: the Pacific Northwest, from British Columbia to northern California. Mole salamanders spend their lives almost entirely underground. They are found in southern Alaska and throughout the U.S. and Mexico. Species in these three families hatch from eggs laid in water, go through a **larval** stage, and then develop into land-dwelling adults. Amphibians are the only **vertebrate** animals that begin life in a larval stage.

The lungless salamander family makes up about 60 percent of all salamander species. These salamanders are found mostly in North America and Europe. They can be distinguished from other salamanders by the small slits between their nostrils and upper lip. These organs are called nasolabial grooves and are used to detect scent. The world's smallest salamanders are lungless salamanders found only in Oaxaca, Mexico. Called minute (*MY-noot*) salamanders, they are about half an inch (1.3 cm) long, and all are endangered. In 2016, 3 new species were classified, bringing the number of minute salamander species to 29. Many lungless species skip the larval stage and hatch as fully formed juvenile salamanders.

Many salamander and newt hatchlings are no bigger than a ladybug—and some are even smaller.

Newt larvae become juveniles called efts that live on land for a few years before growing into aquatic or semiaquatic adults.

While fire salamanders can grow up to 10 inches (25.4 cm) long, they typically weigh no more than a golf ball.

The Salamandridae family includes both terrestrial "true" salamanders and aquatic newts. They are found throughout the northern hemisphere in various habitats, from mountain streams to Greek islands to African plains. They are typically the brightest colored salamanders. Mandarin newts are brown with bright orange or yellow toes, tails, and spots on the ridges along the sides of the head and body. Some fire salamanders are solid yellow, while others are yellow with black spots or stripes. And with high, jagged crests along their backs, male crested newts look like tiny dinosaurs.

Salamanders should not be confused with lizards, which are reptiles. All reptiles have dry, scaly skin. Amphibians lack scales and produce **mucus** to help their smooth skin remain moist. The skin is also permeable, meaning water and gases can pass through it. Salamanders do not drink water. Instead, the skin on a salamander's underside soaks up moisture from the surface on which the animal sits. Salamanders can also breathe—that is, take in oxygen and expel carbon dioxide—through their skin and the tissue that lines their mouths. Because they have no **diaphragm**, terrestrial salamanders that breathe

Eastern newts hatch in the water, live on land as efts for two to three years, and then return to the water for adulthood.

Many salamanders instinctively search for places to hibernate when fall weather arrives.

Male arboreal salamanders have front teeth that protrude beyond the bottom lip, making their bite especially painful.

through their mouths must pump muscles in their throats to force air in and out of their lungs.

As amphibians, salamanders are ectothermic animals. They cannot produce heat to warm themselves the way birds and **mammals** do. Their body temperature depends on the environment, so they must avoid extreme heat and cold. Most salamanders prefer temperatures ranging from 50 to 70 °F (10 to 21 °C), though some remain active down to 32 °F (0 °C). All salamanders need access to water to survive, so most live near streams or ponds. A few species have adapted to arid environments. The Iranian harlequin newt lives in western Iran, where water is available for only a few months each year. These newts feed and mate during the wet season and then burrow underground to **hibernate** during the long dry season. Salamanders dig using the four toes on their front feet and four or five toes on their rear feet. Some salamanders that live in rock crevices and trees have **webbed** feet for gripping flat surfaces.

Because most salamanders are nocturnal, or active at night, their eyes are adapted to seeing in dim light. Salamanders can see color, though they cannot detect

as many variations in color as humans can. Also, salamanders cannot see fine detail. Aquatic salamanders have eyes similar to those of fish. They see mostly changes in light and shadow. Some cave-dwelling salamanders, such as the olm and the Texas blind salamander, exist in complete darkness, so they have no need for vision. Their eyes are just dark spots covered with skin. These salamanders are highly sensitive to changes in water pressure. They can feel when prey—snails, shrimps, and other small creatures—move nearby.

Banded newts belong to a semiaquatic salamander group known as "tritons," named for a Greek god and sea messenger.

Fire salamanders produce venom in special organs behind their eyes and down their backs that damages the nervous systems of attackers.

SWIMMERS, CRAWLERS, AND CLIMBERS

S alamanders are carnivores, meaning they eat other animals. Terrestrial salamanders generally find prey in moist soil or leaf litter or beneath rotting logs and rocks. They mostly eat earthworms, spiders, and small insects. Large salamanders may also prey on frogs, mice, and smaller salamanders. Aquatic salamanders feed on larvae, crayfish, snails, tadpoles, and small fish. Salamanders typically do not chase prey. Instead, they settle in one spot and wait for prey to wander near. Then they shoot their tongues out to nab prey and pull it into their mouths.

The underside of a salamander's tongue is sticky, and its jaws are filled with tiny teeth. Prey has little chance of escape. The various species of mushroomtongue salamanders are named for the fat, fleshy tip of their tongue, and Doflein's salamander is also called the ballistic salamander because its tongue shoots out like a bullet from the barrel of a gun. This salamander has the most powerful tongue of any animal in the world. Its sticky tongue reaches prey in only a few thousandths of a second. It generates 18,000 watts of power per kilogram of muscle. A world-champion bicyclist moving

Sirens use their tiny, paddle-like limbs for swimming rather than walking.

Sirens are the only salamanders known to be omnivorous, eating plant matter and algae in addition to live prey.

Tiger salamanders, which can grow to 14 inches (35.6 cm) long and live up to 25 years, are commonly kept as pets.

at top speed generates less than five watts of power per kilogram of muscle.

Salamanders are typically solitary animals, and many are territorial, meaning they guard a selected area of land or water where they regularly hunt for food. The lungless salamanders defend their territories fiercely. Many other salamander species simply avoid each other. To designate the boundaries of their territories, salamanders use scent marking. All salamanders produce pheromones, which are chemicals that can travel through the air and settle on surfaces. They stimulate various responses in other salamanders. The organ within the nasolabial groove of lungless salamanders is so sensitive to pheromones that individuals can recognize each other by scent.

With few exceptions, salamanders are silent. Some salamanders make a squeaking sound when attacked or handled roughly. A few vocalize regularly. North America's most abundant salamander, the tiger salamander, produces a "blip" sound like a water drop. Some Pacific giant salamanders make a clacking sound. Some newts go "tic-tic-tic." And the arboreal salamander of southern California peeps. Salamanders have internal

ears that can detect sound vibrations, but they do not communicate vocally with each other. Instead, salamanders rely heavily on their pheromones to contact each other during the fall mating season.

All salamanders hatch from eggs. Aquatic species have virtually no contact during mating. They engage in external fertilization of eggs, the way most fish reproduce. In the case of Chinese giant salamanders, the male selects a nest area under a rock in a stream or stream embankment and waits for a female. When she is ready to lay eggs, the female enters the nest area and lays long strands of about 450 jellylike eggs. Then she leaves. The male expels milky sperm over the eggs, fertilizing

Two-lined salamanders are found in New Brunswick, southern Quebec, and everywhere east of the Mississippi except Wisconsin and Michigan.

them. He then stays with the eggs, protecting them from predators until they hatch 10 to 12 weeks later.

Many other salamanders engage in elaborate courtship displays prior to mating. Male newts may show off the crests on their backs or stretch their heads and tails upward to show off colorful undersides. Many male salamanders have a special **gland** under the chin, called a mental gland, which produces pheromones. When a female comes near, the male rubs his chin on the female's head, covering her with pheromones that prompt her to mate. Then the male will drop a jellylike sac containing sperm near the female. This is called a spermatophore, or sperm packet. If the female is sufficiently influenced by the male's courtship displays and pheromones, she will sit on the packet and use her muscles to pull it inside her body through an opening called a cloaca. Other salamander species embrace to mate, with the male holding onto the female with his feet or the two entwining tails so the male can deliver his packet directly into the female's body.

What happens next also varies by family. Some salamanders are ovoviviparous. This means the females produce soft, flexible eggs that are held within the body while the **embryos** inside the eggs develop. The fully formed young hatch before emerging from their mother's body. Other salamanders are oviparous, which means they lay eggs like birds do. But salamander eggs are not hard. They are soft and gummy. Some salamanders lay their eggs in humid places on land buried under rotten leaves, while others lay eggs underwater. The eggs may have sticky threads that anchor them to plants and rocks.

The females of some salamander species are ready to lay their eggs within a few days of mating, while others hold on to the sperm packet for weeks, months, or, in the case of fire salamanders, up to two years. When conditions are favorable, the female allows her eggs

Egg jelly contains substances that help protect eggs from damage and prevent mold from growing.

Many newts lay hundreds of eggs, one at a time, wrapping each in a leaf and using mucus to seal the leaf closed.

Some species exhibit sexual dimorphism, which means males and females differ in size or appearance.

to be fertilized right before laying them. Most female salamanders abandon their eggs after laying them, but some stay nearby to chase away predators. Paddle-tail newts curl up on top of their eggs to protect them.

After hatching from eggs, most salamander larvae are fully aquatic, breathing through gills and equipped with tails for propulsion. Larval forms of salamanders are instant predators, but they do not bite down on prey. Rather, opening their mouths quickly causes a suction that rapidly vacuums up prey, which is swallowed whole. The larvae have gills that eventually disappear when the adult salamander leaves the water for life on land. One exception in the mole salamander family is the critically endangered axolotl of Mexico, which retains its larval form throughout its lifetime. Even terrestrial species such as tiger salamanders may indefinitely remain in their aquatic larval form in habitats where they are not threatened by predatory fish. Most land salamanders live from 5 to 25 years, but members of the giant salamander family can live 50 to 55 years. And scientists recently discovered that olms, whose average life span is 69 years, can live as long as 102 years.

About the length of standard pencils, great crested newts are the largest salamander species in Great Britain.

半上弾正惡弥景

鯱山童子と山椒魚
と云てく
雲州墨油川の
水上天の淵にて
ふれおきくる

In an ancient Japanese tale, samurai hero Hanagami Danjo no jo Arakage battles a giant salamander.

In 1975, Spain made the fire salamander part of a five-stamp collection celebrating amphibians.

F ew animals have a longer or richer history in myth and legend than salamanders. The word "salamander" comes from an Arab-Persian word meaning "lives in fire." The belief that salamanders were born from fire and could survive in fire emerged more than 2,000 years ago. The fourth-century B.C. philosopher Aristotle wrote of the salamander, "this creature, so the story goes, not only walks through the fire but puts it out in doing so." Another early written account of salamanders was published in *Natural History*, an encyclopedia written by Pliny the Elder, an ancient Roman naturalist and author, in A.D. 77. He agreed with Aristotle that salamanders could put out fires with their icy bodies. He then went further in describing a milky venom spewed from the salamander's mouth, which would make a person's hair fall out and cause a skin rash if the substance were touched. He also said that a person would die from eating the meat of an animal, such as a pig, that had previously eaten a salamander.

In the sixth century, the Spanish scholar Isidore of Seville furthered people's fears of salamanders. He wrote that if a salamander climbed a tree, all the fruit of that tree would

A 13th-century British book (left) and a stone sculpture at the French Hôtel de Bourgtheroulde (center) feature salamanders, as does the historic royal palace, Château de Fontainebleau, in France (right).

become poisoned, and if a salamander fell into a well, the water would likewise become poisoned. This belief was carried on through the ages. The 13th-century English writer Bartholomew de Glanville recounted a fable about a salamander that bathed in a river, poisoning it. When the army of Alexander the Great, the ancient Greek conqueror, drank from the river, 4,000 men and 2,000 horses died.

Even during the Renaissance, when people learned a great deal about science and nature, Leonardo da Vinci wrote that the salamander had no digestive organs and ate no food except the fire in which it renewed its scaly skin. In the 16th century, Paracelsus, an **alchemist**, wrote that everything in nature is made from one of four elements:

air, earth, water, and fire. He named the spirits of these elements "elementals." They could take human or animal form. Air spirits were called sylphs, earth spirits were called gnomes, and water spirits were called undines. Salamanders were the physical embodiment of fire spirits. Paracelsus wrote that salamanders dwelled inside volcanoes, spitting rivers of fire down mountainsides.

All such legends likely stemmed from an unfortunate coincidence. Salamanders often hibernate under the loose bark and in the hollow spaces of fallen trees. When people gathered firewood, they probably carried sleeping salamanders into their homes. Then, upon burning the logs, the salamanders awoke and emerged, undoubtedly

Salamanders appear on buildings in Germany (left) and New York City (center); Château de Fontainebleau (right) contains more than 800 salamanders in various media.

THE SALAMANDER

The following is from the "Life of Benvenuto Cellini," an Italian artist of the sixteenth century, written by himself: "When I was about five years of age, my father, happening to be in a little room in which they had been washing, and where there was a good fire of oak burning, looked into the flames and saw a little animal resembling a lizard, which could live in the hottest part of that element...."

It seems unreasonable to doubt a story of which Signor Cellini was both an eye and ear witness. Add to which the authority of numerous sage philosophers, at the head of whom are Aristotle and Pliny, affirms this power of the salamander. According to them, the animal not only resists fire, but extinguishes it, and when he sees the flame charges it as an enemy which he well knows how to vanquish....

The foundation of the above fables is supposed to be the fact that the salamander really does secrete from the pores of his body a milky juice, which when he is irritated is produced in considerable quantity, and would doubtless, for a few moments, defend the body from fire. Then it is a hibernating animal, and in winter retires to some hollow tree or other cavity, where it coils itself up and remains in a torpid state till the spring again calls it forth. It may therefore sometimes be carried with the fuel to the fire, and wake up only time enough to put forth all its faculties for its defence. Its viscous juice would do good service, and all who profess to have seen it, acknowledge that it got out of the fire as fast as its legs could carry it; indeed, too fast for them ever to make prize of one, except in one instance, and in that one the animal's feet and some parts of its body were badly burned.

from Bulfinch's Mythology, *by Thomas Bulfinch (1796–1867)*

startling those who witnessed this "magical" event. Thus, the fire salamanders got their name, and their reputation grew from there. Not only were salamanders believed to be fireproof themselves, but people came to believe that they could provide protection from fire as well. The *Talmud*, an important Jewish text written between A.D. 200 and 500, suggested that a person covered in salamander blood would be safe from fire. Some people believed that salamanders had wool like sheep that could be woven into fireproof garments. Marco Polo, the Italian adventurer who wrote about his travels in Central Asia and China, spread the idea that salamanders were not animals but rather an earthly substance similar to gold that formed in mountains. Called "salamander," this substance was mined and woven into fabric. Researchers today believe that this substance was actually a mineral called asbestos, which forms threadlike crystals. Asbestos is naturally fire retardant. What Marco Polo saw was probably asbestos veins in rock. The fabric made of woven silk and gold that he brought west from China was called salamander skin, and likely contained asbestos fibers. The sticky, foamy mucus produced by some salamanders also could have been used to coat fabric,

Male crested newts develop the jagged crests on their backs during mating season; the crests are then shed and sometimes eaten.

Spanish ribbed newts sent into space were found to regenerate damaged tissues twice as fast as those on Earth.

For defense, the Spanish ribbed newt can rotate its ribs to break through its skin, forming spikes coated with poison.

forming a thick barrier resistant to fire. The 12th-century rabbi Yehudah HaChassid wrote of an incident in which a garment made of salamander "wool" did not burn in a fire until after he washed it. Scientists today think this story could have some basis in fact. Firefighters have recorded instances of salamanders, particularly newts, being covered in thick, foamy mucus and then walking short distances across burning forestland. By the time the salamanders reached safety, the mucus had turned into a hard coating that cracked and crumbled off the amphibians' bodies.

Salamanders' association with fire has remained strong in literature. In the fourth Narnia book by C. S. Lewis, *The Silver Chair* (1953), salamanders are wise beings that live in the flames of Bism, far beneath Underland. In the first book of Piers Anthony's Xanth series, *A Spell for Chameleon* (1977), salamanders breathe magical fire that cannot be extinguished by any normal means, for it even burns water. Salamanders appear as magical creatures in J. K. Rowling's Harry Potter series (1997–2007). The brilliant orange lizards live in fireplaces and die without heat, though rubbing chili pepper over their bodies can protect them. Salamander-like dragons also appear in Tony

DiTerlizzi and Holly Black's the Spiderwick Chronicles (2003–04) and Beyond the Spiderwick Chronicles (2007–09). In the *Spiderwick Chronicles* video games, alchemists can use salamanders' fire to turn lead into gold.

Salamanders appear in countless video and online games. In Blizzard Entertainment's Warcraft franchise, salamanders are 40 feet (12.2 m) long and breathe fire. Pokémon fans will recognize Charmander as a salamander-like character with a flaming tail, just as Digimon fans will be familiar with Salamandermon as a fiery Japanese giant salamander. A variety of salamander heroes and villains appear in such franchises as BattleTech, Mana, and Witcher. Even the DC Comics universe includes a salamander superhero. As one of the four Elementals, Ginger O'Shea's body was taken over by a fire spirit and became Salamander, a character that can transform into a flaming mass. She debuted in 1978 with the three other Elementals, Gnome, Sylph, and Undine. They joined the Justice League and fought crime alongside other superheroes. The long tradition of magic and mystery surrounding salamanders continues to bring these creatures to life in an endless array of unique characters.

A salamander fountain stands in Perpignan, a city in southern France that was founded in the 10th century.

The number of Chinese giant salamanders in the wild has declined by more than 80 percent since the 1960s.

OLDEST ANIMALS ON LAND

Amphibians were the first animals to **evolve** from fish and invade land about 365 million years ago—roughly 135 million years before the first dinosaurs appeared. *Acanthostega* is the oldest known amphibian. Its fossilized remains were found in Greenland, which was a lush swamp at the time it lived. *Acanthostega* was about six feet (1.8 m) long and looked somewhat like the modern Chinese giant salamander. Because it had no elbows or knees, it could not walk and instead had to drag itself with its limbs. Fossils of the largest amphibian ever, *Prionosuchus*, were found in Brazil. This creature lived 250 million years ago and grew up to 30 feet (9.1 m) long. It lived in shallow lagoons, sharing its habitat with primitive sharks and lungfishes—fish that could breathe air. As competition for food and the need to hide from predators increased, amphibians became much smaller. Fossils of the oldest salamander were found in China in 2012. *Beiyanerpeton jianpingensis* lived 157 million years ago. It was about six inches (15.2 cm) long and had gills, making it similar in size and appearance to today's dwarf waterdog.

Studies on garter snakes show some have adapted a tolerance to salamander **toxin**, allowing them to eat salamanders.

Salamanders have survived so long because of their remarkable ability to adapt to changing conditions, but this may not be enough to save them in the future. In recent decades, salamanders have suffered under a number of environmental pressures that, intensified by human activity, threaten to devastate their populations. According to the International Union for Conservation of Nature (IUCN), more than 70 salamander species are currently critically endangered. This is the highest risk category assigned by the IUCN Red List of Threatened Species. Habitat destruction, pollution, **poaching**, and disease are all to blame.

A serious disease-related threat is chytridiomycosis (*ki-TRI-dee-o-my-KO-sis*), or chytrid fungus. This disease, which can affect any amphibian, destroys salamanders' skin, inhibiting respiration and slowly suffocating the animals. Not much is known about the disease, and since the mid-1900s, it has spread rapidly around the globe, decreasing many salamander populations.

One species that has scientists and conservations highly concerned is the axolotl. **Captive-reared** axolotls are bred as research subjects and pets, but wild axolotls are now extremely rare. Listed as a vulnerable species since 1996,

only 2,000 axolotls were left in the wild by 2004. Because of severe water pollution in their last remaining habitat, the lakes and canals of Xochimilco (*SOH-chee-MIL-ko*), a suburb of Mexico City, their numbers continued to plummet. In 2006, they were listed as critically endangered. In 2013, after spending months searching for axolotls in the wild, scientists could find none and feared they had gone **extinct**. Then, early in 2014, a team of researchers from the National Autonomous University of Mexico led by biologist Armando Tovar Garza found

Fewer than 100 axolotls are believed to exist in Xochimilco, making the threat of their extinction in the wild imminent.

Japanese giant salamanders have a single lung, which they use to raise and lower themselves in the water.

two axolotls. Despite attempts to create protected areas for axolotls in Xochimilco, pollution, invasive species, and urban development are quickly driving these salamanders toward extinction. Releasing captive-reared axolotls is not an option for species recovery because disease and mutations could occur. Similarly, captive populations suffer from a lack of **genetic** diversity and likely will not provide a lasting conservation solution.

In 2004, scientists witnessed the gradual extinction of the Yunnan Lake newt, which inhabited the shores of Kunming Lake in the Chinese province of Yunnan. Only one inch (2.5 cm) long, this salamander was helpless against growing Chinese urbanization and industrialization. The IUCN reported that the Yunnan Lake newt fell victim to "general pollution, land reclamation, domestic duck farming, and the introduction of exotic fish and frog species." Scientists speculate that many species disappear without notice because they may die off before humans get the chance to discover them.

Conservation efforts have long been underway for the Japanese giant salamander. In Japan, this salamander is considered a natural treasure. There it is called *osanshouo* (*OH-sahn-SHOW-oh-wa*) and has been protected by law for more than 50 years. The Hiroshima Asa Zoological Park was the first to develop a successful **captive-breeding** program, and, in 2010, the zoo donated five salamanders to the National Zoo in Washington, D.C., in order to begin a breeding program in the U.S. One of the salamanders died in 2016, but the project has continued.

More extensive still is the decades-long research on how olms can navigate and find food in their pitch-dark environments. The National Center for Scientific Research (CNRS) in France founded a field station in Moulis in 1948. Located underground, it is the oldest and largest cave laboratory in the world. In the 1950s,

The Doflein's salamander of Central America can thrust its tongue forward 50 times faster than the blink of an eye.

The hellbender is found only in mountainous forests from southern New York to northeastern Mississippi.

North America's largest salamander, the hellbender, grows up to 29 inches (73.7 cm) long and weighs up to 5.5 pounds (2.5 kg).

Yugoslavia's president Josip Tito presented French president Charles de Gaulle with some olms for study in France's research cave. Today's olms are the descendants of Tito's gift. In the 1960s, a similar cave laboratory opened in what is now Slovenia. The laboratory serves as a sanctuary for injured olms that are washed out of their caves during seasonal flooding. Scientists also study the olms and breed them in this natural environment. In 2002, a subspecies of dark-skinned olm emerged and has become part of the research. Scientists believe that olms use Earth's **magnetic field** to find their way around, perhaps with the aid of magnetoreception. This is a sense that allows an animal to detect a magnetic field and thus perceive its orientation and direction in a given space. The source of this ability is not certain, but scientists think it could be related to a substance called magnetite, a mineral that is found in the bodies of some animals.

Salamander losses could be greater than people realize. Though salamanders are safe to touch, they should never be eaten, for they are all poisonous to ingest in varying degrees. The rough-skinned newt, found on the Pacific coast of the U.S. and British Columbia, has enough poison

in its body to kill 12 adults if eaten. Understood and used properly, such powerful toxins could actually help humans. More than 200 chemical toxins that are beneficial in medical research have already been discovered from just a small percentage of the world's amphibians. Salamanders are important members of often-fragile **ecosystems**. These amazing creatures can never be replaced once driven to extinction. To preserve salamanders for future generations and discover the secrets they hold, we must take serious steps toward conserving them today.

The rough-skinned newt's toxin blocks nerve impulses that make the lungs work, causing victims to stop breathing.

ANIMAL TALE: HOW SALAMANDER GOT HIS SPOTS

Many American Indian legends were traditionally told to explain how things in the world came to be. This story from the Catawba people of the region that now includes North and South Carolina tells how many animals, including the eastern tiger salamander, came to look the way they do. The legend also features the Yehasuri (*YAY-hah-SOO-ree*). These fairy-like nature spirits are mischief-makers.

Long ago, all the animals were dark-colored and plain. One day, to celebrate the most beautiful summer sunrise ever made, the Creator decreed that all the living creatures would dip paintbrushes in the glorious sunrise and paint each other with the brilliant colors. Everyone grew excited. Salamander was especially thrilled, for he loved to paint.

Salamander rushed to dip his brush in the sunrise. "Let me paint you, Woodpecker," he called out.

Woodpecker flew down, and Salamander began painting his head a brilliant red color. Just then, the Yehasuri appeared. They engaged Salamander in a game, distracting him from his work. "I must paint Woodpecker," Salamander told them. The Yehasuri pulled some white clouds from the sky and tossed them at Woodpecker. "Good enough!" they cried, and before long, Salamander and the Yehasuri were dancing and laughing. Tired of waiting, Woodpecker flew away. This is why woodpeckers are black and white with red on their heads.

Suddenly, Salamander remembered that he was supposed to be painting. He dipped his brush in the sunrise again and ran to Blackbird. "Let me paint you yellow and red," he called out. "Yes, yes!" said Blackbird. Salamander began painting Blackbird's wings. But once again, the Yehasuri engaged Salamander in play.

Blackbird, tired of waiting for Salamander to finish, flew away. This is why some blackbirds have yellow and red on their wings.

Salamander once again realized that he should be painting, not playing. He called out to Snake, "Let me paint you bright orange." Snake slithered over to Salamander, who dipped his brush in the sunrise. "You will be beautiful," Salamander said to Snake. But Salamander had no sooner made a single mark on Snake than the Yehasuri dragged him away to dance and sing. Snake slithered away. This is why ring-necked snakes are dark with a narrow orange ring around their necks.

When Mole appeared, Salamander again remembered that he was supposed to be painting. "Come, Mole," he called. "I will paint you a beautiful pink color." Salamander dipped his brush in the sunrise and went to work. He painted Mole's feet and long claws. Then he painted Mole's nose. But before he could continue, Salamander found himself lured into a game with the Yehasuri. Tired of being ignored, Mole shuffled away. This is why moles are dark with pink feet and noses.

Salamander had been so busy painting other creatures and playing with the Yehasuri that he did not stop to get painted himself. Now the sun had climbed high in the sky, and the sunrise colors were almost gone. A little bit of yellow was all that was left. "Oh, please," cried Salamander. "Won't somebody paint me?" After all their mischief, the Yehasuri took pity on Salamander. Racing up to the last remnants of the sunrise, they grabbed the yellow color. Then they sprinkled it over Salamander. This is why the eastern tiger salamander is dark with yellow spots.

GLOSSARY

adapted – changed to improve its chances of survival in its environment

alchemist – an ancient chemist who was concerned with understanding changes in the properties of matter

aquatic – living or growing in water

captive-breeding – being bred and raised in a place from which escape is not possible

captive-reared – raised in a place from which escape is not possible

diaphragm – a dome-shaped, muscular structure in the chest that contracts to inflate the lungs

ecosystems – communities of organisms that live together in environments

embryos – unborn or unhatched offspring in the early stages of development

evolve – to gradually develop into a new form

extinct – having no living members

genetic – relating to genes, the basic physical units of heredity

gills – body parts that extract oxygen from water

gland – an organ in a human or animal body that produces chemical substances used by other parts of the body

hibernate – to spend the winter in a sleeplike state in which breathing and heart rate slow down

larval – describing the phase of a newly hatched, immature form of an animal before it grows into a completely different adult form

magnetic field – the invisible force that makes compass needles line up in a north-south direction

mammals – warm-blooded animals that have a backbone and hair or fur, give birth to live young, and produce milk to feed their young

mucus – a sticky or slimy substance secreted by glands or organs in a living thing

mythical – relating to a collection of myths, or popular, traditional beliefs or stories that explain how something came to be or that are associated with a person or object

organ – part of a living being that exists to perform a specific task in the living being's body

poaching – hunting protected species of wild animals, even though doing so is against the law

toxin – a substance that is harmful or poisonous

vertebrate – an animal that has a backbone, including mammals, birds, reptiles, amphibians, and fish

webbed – connected by a web (of skin, as in the case of webbed feet)

SELECTED BIBLIOGRAPHY

"Barred Tiger Salamander." Smithsonian's National Zoo & Conservation Biology Institute. https://nationalzoo.si.edu/animals/barred-tiger-salamander.

Heying, Heather. "*Salamandridae* – Newts, Salamanders." Animal Diversity Web. http://animaldiversity.org/accounts/Salamandridae/.

Larson, Allan, David Wake, and Tom Devitt. "Caudata – Salamanders." Tree of Life Web Project. http://tolweb.org/Caudata/14939.

Naish, Darren. "The Amazing World of Salamanders." *Scientific American*. https://blogs.scientificamerican.com/tetrapod-zoology/the-amazing-world-of-salamanders/.

Petranka, James W. *Salamanders of the United States and Canada*. 2nd ed. Washington, D.C.: Smithsonian Books, 2010.

Sparreboom, Max. *Salamanders of the Old World: The Salamanders of Europe, Asia and Northern Africa*. Zeist, The Netherlands: KNNV, 2014.

Note: Every effort has been made to ensure that any websites listed above were active at the time of publication. However, because of the nature of the Internet, it is impossible to guarantee that these sites will remain active indefinitely or that their contents will not be altered.

Because salamanders are so secretive, spotting one in the wild is considered a rare treat.

INDEX